THE

NEW-FASHIONED
WEDDING

THE
NEW-FASHIONED
WEDDING

DESIGNING YOUR

Artful, Modern, Crafty, Textured, Sophisticated Celebration

PAIGE APPEL & KELLY HARRIS

Written with Shoko Wanger

RIZZOLI
NEW YORK

New York · Paris · London · Milan

THANK YOU SO MUCH. WE COULDN'T DO IT WITHOUT YOU.
YOU KNOW WHO YOU ARE.

Chris, Kevin, Irene, Jean Ellen, Mark, Jerry, Richard, Julie, Annie M, Melissa, Laurel, Kelly C, Annie T, Talmadge, Michael, Brian, Max, Margaux, Shoko, Noa, Britni, Charley, Matt, Sarah, Melody, Ashley, Pappin, Geoff, Kelty, Hannah, Dominique, Ron, Rob, Jaimi, Bonnie, Jen, Kelly E, Taneka, Alli, Jeni, Bri, Nyrie, Jonathan, Jared, Reiko, Loop, Diana, Josh, Keith, Lisa, Amanda, Kristina, Jillian, Jill, Leora, Smiles, Jason, Robert, Gary, Jihan, Jessica, Emarie, Liz, Audrey, Clover, Jennifer, Remy, Millie, and Pickle.

And big thanks to all of our brides and grooms, in this book and out. We have loved designing your weddings.

LOVE, PAIGE & KELLY

First published in the United States of America in 2012
by Rizzoli International Publications, Inc.
300 Park Avenue South
New York, NY 10010
www.rizzoliusa.com

Designed by Headcase Design
www.headcasedesign.com

2012 2013 2014 2015 / 10 9 8 7 6 5 4 3 2 1

Distributed in the U.S. trade by
Random House, New York

Printed in China

ISBN-13: 978-0-8478-3988-9

Library of Congress Catalog Control Number:
2012946456

PHOTO CREDITS

Front cover photos:
Top: Max Wanger
Bottom: Birds of a Feather Photography

Back cover photos:
Top: Featherlove Photogrpahy
Middle: Max Wanger
Bottom: Bonnie Tsang

Pages 1, 4, 8: Max Wanger,

Page 2: Love Me Sailor Photography,

Page 6: FeatherLove Photography

Pages 14, 15 (horse), 36, 56, 86, 108, 126, 146, 162, 163 (small book), 184, 206 (buttons): Annie McElwain, www.anniemcelwain.com

Chapter 1: Birds of a Feather Photography)

Chapter 2: Charley*Star (except page 37, rug photo, Casa de Perrin)

Chapter 3: Max Wanger

Chapter 4: Featherlove Photography

Chapter 5: Love Me Sailor Photography

Chapter 6: Max Wanger

Chapter 7: Weaver House

Chapter 8: Charley*Star

Chapter 9: Max Wanger

Chapter 10: Bonnie Tsang

CONTENTS

FOREWORD

We came to know Paige and Kelly as their partnership was just beginning to form, and our site and blog were just taking off. From the beginning, it's been clear that these women have a vision that is different and progressive and exceptional. Their ability to transform simple, often humble materials into complex projects and installations is a constant source of inspiration to so many people in the industry, as well as to their lucky clients.

As bloggers and curators of inspiration, we are always thrilled to see new work from Bash, Please come our way. Their distinct approach to design mixes rustic and modern, indie cool with sophistication and charm . . . it's a brilliant mash-up of all that's great from so many different styles. They have a special ability to transform something old into something new, to make the expected a surprise again, and to present an idea we thought we'd seen too many times in an entirely innovative way. They are always thinking, always designing, always challenging themselves to be more creative than they already are. And that's what makes good designers truly great.

Since it's known that they have exceptional taste, it's in everyone's best interest to pay attention when they've introduced a new idea or creative partner to the broader community. Their production of the popular Cream Event twice a year has further elevated their influence on event design. They not only do a bang-up job of promoting their own impressive work, but they are tireless in their efforts to bring ideas and festivities to all couples looking for inspiration, not just those who are lucky enough to work with them. And as regular participants in The Cream, we can vouch for the fact that a Bash, Please event is ALWAYS a good time.

Above all else we can say that the work that Bash, Please turns out has transformed and tightened the community here in Los Angeles, and encouraged creative people in this industry everywhere to look beyond what's expected for new and even more exceptional ways to create experiences that celebrate the joys of life.

We promise that this book will provide all the inspiration you need to envision an event you're planning. Or perhaps you're just hoping to get lost in the beautiful daydream. We'd recommend that too.

xoxo
Jillian Clark, Amanda Halbrook,
Kristina Meltzer
100layercake.com

INTRODUCTION

Neither of us ever thought we'd be where we are today.

We weren't starry-eyed little girls who day-dreamed about our wedding days. We weren't peppy college ingenues aspiring to be party planners. We weren't twenty-something job seekers sending resumes to David Tutera and Mindy Weiss. Nope. Until we met one fateful day over coffee in Los Angeles, we were on very different paths.

And yet, here we are. Best friends, business partners, proud owners of an event-production business—and, now, authors of a book. We're on a mission to create what we like to call "new-fashioned" weddings: barnyards over ballrooms; linen over polyester; wildflowers over red roses; vibrant, seasonal cuisine over standard catered fare. After all, our clients are modern, hip, and design-conscious—they're "new-fashioned" themselves.

You may be wondering whether there's a formula we adhere to when we approach wedding design, some sort of proven method for finding inspiration or making our clients' ideas come to life. In fact, there isn't. Years of experience have taught us that the most heartfelt events are the ones that come together thoughtfully and organically. The ideas strike when you least expect them.

If you're planning a wedding and don't know where to start, here's our advice: gather inspiration from a variety of sources. Visit art museums, page through design magazines, browse the window displays of your favorite shops. Wander flea markets, pore over art books, peruse Pinterest, travel.

Above all, think about what's meaningful to you. Do you prefer Ralph Lauren or Rodarte? Potted cacti or peonies? Sam Cooke or Carla Bruni? Champagne or tequila?

Whether it's an intimate ceremony in a quiet neighborhood park or a weekend-long extravaganza at a hip hotel, your wedding should make you happy. When all's said and done, it's simple: the day should be about *you*.

We hope the weddings featured on these pages will inspire you to think adventurously. Color outside the lines. Approach your big day with a sense that anything is possible in a new-fashioned world.

One last bit of advice? Don't forget to enjoy yourself. (That's the most important part.)

Love,
Paige and Kelly

COUNTRY ECLECTIC

JESSICA & JOE

"WHAT DO YOU CALL THE UNION BETWEEN A JEWISH BRIDE AND A CATHOLIC GROOM? A CASHEW, OF COURSE!"

When Jessica uttered these words at our first meeting at the Culver Hotel, we had a hunch that we were in for some fun. And we were right. Rife with personal details—hand-knit *kippot*, a klezmer band, wine labels bearing the playful moniker "Joessica"—Jessica and Joe's Palos Verdes, California, farm wedding was the perfect blend of two very vivacious personalities. Two hundred and fifty guests in a corral with red-hot juleps, wildflowers galore, a mouth-watering "Sweets Stable," and a dance floor—what's not to love?

VISION STATEMENT:

European farmhouse meets California vineyard. A sweet wedding combining the eclectic sensibilities of a rustic, alfresco dinner with the poise of an upscale private estate wedding.

KEY WORDS:

Warm, bountiful, sophisticated.

CHATTER:

Jessica: I want an intimate evening with an alfresco dinner party, lots of wood and wildflowers, and dancing till dawn.

Us: Of course you do. What's your guest count?

Jessica: Two hundred and fifty.

Us: Well, if your parents' corral is big enough to accommodate that number, we'll figure out how to make it feel cozy.

Jessica: We also want to incorporate Portuguese music, our love of sweets, and both a Catholic priest and a rabbi. Oh, and spicy cocktails, too.

Us: Spicy cocktails and Portuguese music sound right up our alley.

Jessica: I also want to be best friends with you after the wedding.

Us: Done.

air plants

canning jars

freshly baked pies

café lights

country fabrics

barnyard setting

Guests dined
and danced under
a starlit sky.

ELEMENTS

opposite, 1 **PAPER GOODS**
Custom details included an exquisite, boldly-printed invitation suite and a large poster (used in lieu of a traditional guest book) that was silk-screened to resemble tree rings.

2, 3 **HAND-KNIT** *KIPPOT*
Handmade by the mother of the groom, these knitted *kippot* in cornflower blue doubled as wedding favors. "Celebrating our interfaith marriage took a lot of understanding and patience from both sides of our family," says Jessica. "Having Maria hand-knit the *kippot* meant that my future mother-in-law embraced my Jewish heritage. It meant the world to me, and to us." Tiny silver cups held bobby pins to fasten the *kippot* in place. As a special touch, we tied hand-torn strips of chambray (a design element we incorporated throughout the event) around each one.

ATTIRE & FLOWERS

1 HEADBAND
To match the *chuppah*, the flower girl's headband was wrapped in simple cotton grosgrain ribbon and fashioned with a similar mix of blooms—Dahlia, kangaroo paw, and wax flower.

2 BRIDESMAID BOUQUET
Bridesmaids carried small, hand-tied posies made of pink Astilbe.

3 BOUTS
Terracotta saucers cradled boutonnieres that were handcrafted using green Ranunculus, kangaroo paw, Dahlia, and exploding grass.

4 *CHUPPAH* FLOWERS
Dahlia, King Protea, Craspedia, and kangaroo paw made for a stunning topper on the *chuppah* (which, sweetly enough, was hand-built by Jessica's father). Heirloom roses cut from the family garden provided an additional personal touch.

5 BRIDAL BOUQUET
Gorgeous, green-centered roses were the centerpiece for Jessica's bouquet. We wanted it to appear as if it had been picked from a field of wildflowers.

6 HAIR
The bride wore her hair in a romantic braided chignon. Sweet, simple, and elegant.

7 DRESS
We loved the way the intricate beading on the sleeves of Jessica's Reem Acra gown caught the sunlight with her every move.

FOOD AND DRINK

opposite **PLACE CARDS**
A farmyard woodpile—already on-site when we arrived—proved to be an ideal spot to hang our tea-stained place cards. (The cards were beautifully hand-lettered by calligrapher Jill Velez.) A scattering of wildflowers was all we needed to dress it up for the festivities.

1 APPETIZERS
Savory appetizers from Heirloom LA included BLT wraps, butternut squash agnolotti with brown butter and sage, and our personal favorite, these purple potatoes, which were twice-baked and topped with crème fraîche.

2 FOOD
After the ceremony, guests nibbled on a summery spread that featured flatbread pizzas, crostini, pickled veggies, and a selection of gourmet meats and cheeses.

3 FOOD LABELS
The names of menu items were written on square slates in colored chalk.

1

2

3

4

1 FLORA

We spruced up rustic wooden tables with boatloads of flowers and plants: maidenhair ferns, Ranunculus, Craspedia, King Protea, and kangaroo paw. To avoid an overly stylized setup, we used an assortment of vintage bottles, mason jars, and patined flower pots that we had sourced from flea markets, Etsy shops, specialty rental companies, and our own in-office collection. We're also expert recyclers: that tall wooden box in the back is an old wine crate that we repurposed as a planter.

2 MENUS

The bar menu was displayed in a simple, blonde-wood frame amid a scattering of air plants and potted greenery. One extra-special detail that we loved: We scanned in the chambray fabric that we used for the dinner napkins to create the illusion of a clothlike texture in the font.

3 BEER TUB

We spotted this claw-foot bathtub on the farm and knew we needed to find a way to incorporate it into the event. Inspiration struck: why not turn it into a beer cooler? One hand-painted sign and a few King Protea later, and the transformation was complete.

4, 5 RED HOT JULEP

Cocktail mastermind Talmadge Lowe, of Pharmacie, combined bourbon, sugar, mint, and jalapeño to make these fiery cocktails. We loved the dried chili pepper garnish. Other beverages on offer included lemonade, as well as sweet vermouth with lemon, lime, and orange.

1

2

3

1 TABLESCAPE

On top of each dinner plate was a bottle of wine made from grapes grown on the bride's family's vineyard. For added tabletop flair, we cut napkins from an assortment of different fabrics: chambray, natural linen, farm floral, and marigold print. Sweet and easygoing, the napkins allowed us to keep the table settings casual without sacrificing style.

2, 3 FLOWER ARRANGEMENTS

We laid linen runners down the center of the dining tables and used glass bottles and patined flower pots in a variety of shapes, sizes, and colors to hold lush greenery and succulents. Votive candles, potted cacti, and air plants—one of our favorite all-natural decorations—filled in the empty spaces. The overall effect was fresh, summery, wild, and charmingly picnic-like.

"TRUE LOVE IS A BIG DEAL"

The bottles of wine were wrapped inside custom screen-printed tote bags emblazoned with the couple's names and wedding date, along with a message that held deep personal meaning. "At our engagement party, Joe made a toast that brought us all to tears," Jessica remembers. "At the end, he looked at me and said, 'True love is a big deal.' That simple phrase stuck with me, because our love is exactly that—a big deal, and true." We stenciled table numbers onto tall glass water bottles and created special Bride and Groom place cards using chalkboard paint and a chalk pen.

opposite **SWEETS**
A "Sweets Stable" (abundantly supplied by L.A. bakery Cake Monkey) played host to peanut butter cake, inside-out s'mores, and a wide array of other bite-size treats. We made decorative garlands using leftover fabric from the dinner napkins.

1 PIES
In addition to wedding cake, guests were offered an assortment of Heirloom LA–made pies in seven flavors, including strawberry, blueberry, lemon meringue, and peach. Perfect pleasures for an early summer celebration.

2, 3 DOGGIE BAGS
Gocco-printed paper doggie bags were available for guests who craved a snack or two for the ride home—or a pastry for the next morning's breakfast. (Shh, we won't tell.)

CHAPTER
{ № 2 }

BACKYARD
BOHEMIAN

ANNA & COLBY

ANNA AND COLBY'S WEDDING WAS A TRUE REFLECTION
OF THEIR CALIFORNIA ROOTS. THERE WAS SUNSHINE,
LOCAL INDIE MUSIC, AND A BAJA-INSPIRED FEAST.

There were ferns, vintage china, mismatched chairs, and a custom-painted *chuppah*
made of raw muslin. The bride, naturally, wore blossoms in her hair. But the real icing
on the wildflower-festooned cake was a parade, from the ceremony at a neighborhood
park to the reception at the home of Anna's parents. Guests shook tambourines, blew
bubbles, and waved flags, singing and cheering all the way. We couldn't imagine a
sweeter celebration if we tried.

VISION STATEMENT:

Coastal craftsman meets Navajo Americana. A joyful, organic affair reflecting the couple's West Coast roots and distinctive, free-spirited style.

KEY WORDS:

Laid-back, bohemian, California cool.

CHATTER:

Anna: I've done a lot of thinking about my wedding, and here's what I know for sure: I don't want matchy-matchy bridesmaids or a hotel ballroom.

Us: Why would you?

Anna: I'd rather get married guerrilla-style, in the park down the street from my parents' house.

Us: Brilliant. We can stake the *chuppah* the morning of, and after the vows, your guests can parade back to the house.

Anna: I've met with several other wedding planners, and no one seems to share my sensibilities. But seeing the geodes and the succulents around your office, I think you get it.

Us: Amethyst or kyanite?

Anna: Kyanite. Definitely.

Us: Let's incorporate blue into your color palette.

Anna: My favorite color. You're hired.

hand embroidery

summery refreshments

bells & whistles

denim patchwork

vintage rugs

Anna and Colby's table
settings were full of
handmade details.

BOUQUETS & BOUTS

1

2

1 BRIDAL BOUQUET

Anna's bouquet—which included blue thistle, Amaranthus, and echinacea—was bound with strips of denim. "I wanted the flowers to look as though they had been picked from my mother's garden, where we had the party," she says. Braided hair, a floral headband, and a pair of sky-blue heels completed her breezy, bohemian look.

2 BRIDESMAID BOUQUETS

Anna's bridesmaids—her sister and sister-in-law-to-be—carried sweet pampas grass posies. We loved their unpretentious, field-fresh look. Anna did, too. "I wanted them to feel like they might have been gathered on the way to the ceremony. Nothing too fussy." (Fun fact: all of the bouquets and boutonnieres were tied with denim. We used the leftovers, along with a bit of muslin, to create festive flags for the post-ceremony parade.)

3 BOUTS

The boutonnieres (which we displayed before the ceremony on a vintage wooden tray) contained a cool-blue mix of thistle, lavender, and wax flower buds. For the fathers of the bride and groom, we added sprigs of kangaroo paw for a bright-red accent.

ELEMENTS

1

opposite **CHUPPAH** FLOWERS
We decorated the *chuppah* with many
of the same blooms as we did the bridal
bouquet, embellishing the front with a
length of passion vine.

1 LOGO
The *chuppah* featured a one-of-a-kind
logo by Thunderwing Press, created
using Anna and Colby's initials. (The logo
appeared on the couple's invitation suite,
as well.)

2 VINTAGE CAR
The bride was escorted to the ceremony
in a cream-colored vintage Volvo, on loan
for the day from a friend of the family.

2

LOUNGE

1

2

1 SEATING

Our inspiration for the lounge seating was mid-century modern meets classic Americana. Yeah! Rentals provided furniture and décor, including throw pillows, Eames wooden lounge chairs, and a Case Study couch.

2 RUGS

Vintage kilim and Moroccan-style rugs sourced by Casa de Perrin were layered in the lounge and dining areas. An assortment of colors, patterns, and designs contributed to a funky, folksy look.

3 DÉCOR

A wood slab on a sturdy wire base (also furnished by Yeah! Rentals) held a camping tin filled with autumnal flora: echinacea, King Protea, and trailing passion vine.

4 VINTAGE RECORDS

In addition to a rousing performance by local indie band The Living Sisters, DJs Jimi Hey and Ian Marshall of Wombleton Records spun vintage tunes late into the night.

TABLESCAPE

opposite **DINNER SEATING**
We curated an eclectic assortment of stylish chairs, strung café lights from the rafters, and covered the swimming pool with wood planks and throw rugs to accommodate extra seating.

1 PLACE SETTINGS
In the weeks leading up to the wedding, Anna and her mother trawled the aisles of several Los Angeles flea markets for vintage napkins to use for dinner table place settings. We assembled garden seed packets—tomatoes, carrots, and peas— to place on top, along with letterpressed place cards, designed and calligraphed by Thunderwing Press.

2 BRIDE & GROOM CHAIRS
Blue seemed like a natural choice when it came to deciding on Anna and Colby's color scheme. These knotted denim garlands were made from a few scraps of muslin and bits of extra material from the table runners. Strung from a pair of dinner chairs—hers a hairpin Bentwood, his a shiny Marais A Side—they were a unique and attractive way to designate the bride and groom's places at the table.

1

2

3

1, 2 CENTERPIECES

We used metal camping tins filled with flowers; potted cacti; and single-stem blossoms in vintage amber bottles as centerpieces. "I wanted the flowers to reflect the California vibe that was the backdrop for our entire day," Anna says. Table arrangements echoed those found on the *chuppah*, boutonnieres, and bridal bouquets and featured pampas grass, heirloom roses, thistle, Amaranthus, and passion vine.

3 DENIM TABLECLOTHS

Anna and her friends sewed these one-of-a-kind patchwork runners from scraps of salvaged denim and an old collection of A.P.C. jeans. "We had an assembly line going. A few friends cut, one friend ironed, and the rest of us applied patches. It was so much fun."

4 TABLE NUMBERS

Borrowing elements from Anna and Colby's Thunderwing Press paper goods, we embroidered these table numbers ourselves using hard-to-miss raspberry-colored thread. (We printed out the numbers and designs, attached them to the wooden hoops, and embroidered right on top.) All that needlework made our fingers ache, but in the end, we agreed that the final products were well worth the effort.

FOOD & DRINK

1, 2 APPETIZERS

Heirloom LA honored the couple's love of Mexican food with a colorful spread that included pumpkin empanadas with homemade crème fraîche, brown-butter cactus agnolotti, and purple *chili rellenos* (stuffed chiles) with cheddar, roasted cauliflower, and *queso fresco*.

3 BAR MENU

The bar menu, which we designed using elements pulled from the couple's Thunderwing Press invitation suite, offered a drink called "The Colby," made with Maker's Mark and Mexican Coke.

4 DRINKS

In addition to beer, wine, and champagne, guests sipped vividly hued margaritas in warm-weather flavors like watermelon-jalapeño and blueberry. Ice-cold and garnished with fresh citrus, they were lovely to look at—and sublimely refreshing.

SWEETS TABLE

1

2

1 THE LIVING SISTERS
After the ceremony, friends and family paraded from the park to Anna's parents' house for cocktails. Led by the Living Sisters, guests carried flags, pounded on tambourines, danced their hearts out, and sang at the top of their lungs—truly a sight we'll never forget.

2 TAMBOURINES
Tambourines and kazoos left over from the parade added to the dance-floor fun. (We ordered them from a music store in different shades of blue.)

opposite **CAKE**
When it came to food, southern California flavors rang true, right down to the final course. Among the Heirloom LA sweets on offer: fresh melon, papaya, and pineapple with cayenne pepper, salt, and lime; chipotle Oreos with a spicy buttercream filling; and *tres leches* cake. The triple-flavor wedding cake, created by Vanilla Bake Shop in Santa Monica, featured a colorful array of wildflowers and a lovely (and edible!) rope trim. "The cake was beautiful and, most important, delicious," Anna says.

MODERN
GRAND

JESSICA & AARON

FEATHERED-ARROW ESCORT CARDS, A BOURBON-SOAKED RETRO COCKTAIL HOUR, COLOSSAL BALLOONS, AND A MARCHING BAND. FOR JESSICA AND AARON, CREATIVITY—AND AN ELEMENT OF SURPRISE—HEADLINED THE AGENDA.

(Hardly a shock, given that they both belong to the groundbreaking team that founded Facebook.) From fawning over fonts to choosing just the right style of dinner chair, nary a perfectly polished stone was left unturned. The Ace Hotel in Palm Springs, California—with its youthful, Western frontier atmosphere—was theirs alone for not one but five major events over the course of a spectacular wedding weekend. A dream come true for design devotees like us.

VISION STATEMENT:

Desert modernism meets unfettered whimsy. A spectacular, grandiose, yet still 100 percent personal weekend, carefully considered, down to the last glittering touch.

KEY WORDS:

Vibrant, glamorous, detail oriented.

CHATTER:

Jessica: When it comes to ideas, I've got tons. What I need help with is editing. Look, I've set up about half a dozen blogs and inspiration boards for us to work with.

Us: Wow. There are hundreds of photos and ideas to catalog here. We think you'll need more than one wedding.

Jessica: I agree.

Us: Well, it's a good thing we've got more than one event to plan. How about incorporating your love of vintage into the welcome party and a desert motif into the brunch? Oh, and we'll throw in a swimming pool, too, just to add a little splash.

Jessica: Perfect. And what about custom key cards, too? I was thinking maybe twenty different designs.

Us: Wow again.

Jessica: I want everything thought out. Every little detail.

Us: Will you marry us?

Jessica: Can I work for you?

Us: Sounds like a match made in heaven.

colorful matchbooks

metallic animals

bourbon galore

dapper duds

lively tabletops

Happy and high-spirited,
Jessica and Aaron's
merrymaking knew no
bounds.

DAY 1 | THE HOTEL

1

1 ACE HOTEL
Jessica and Aaron chose the fashionable Ace Hotel & Swim Club in Palm Springs, California, as the setting for their epic, three-day-long celebration.

2 POSTERS
Each hotel room was decorated with three specially designed posters that featured patterns inspired by the desert terrain. (All of Jessica and Aaron's patterned paper

goods were created by Robert and Gary Williams, a sibling design team who also happen to be close friends of the couple's.)

3 WELCOME BAGS
Plastic dinosaur planters (complete with miniature succulents) accompanied silk-screened welcome bags filled with sunscreen, magazines such as *Apartamento* and *The Gentlewoman*, beach towels, and other celebratory necessities.

4 CDS
Mix CDs—with playlists compiled by the Flashdance's Michael Antonia— were housed in vibrant gold-foil cases.

5 "YOU'VE GOT MAIL"
Drawstring sacks hung from the hotel room doors. Each morning, guests would find information about the day's activities tucked inside.

3

4

5

You've got mail!

BOURBON AND BOWTIES

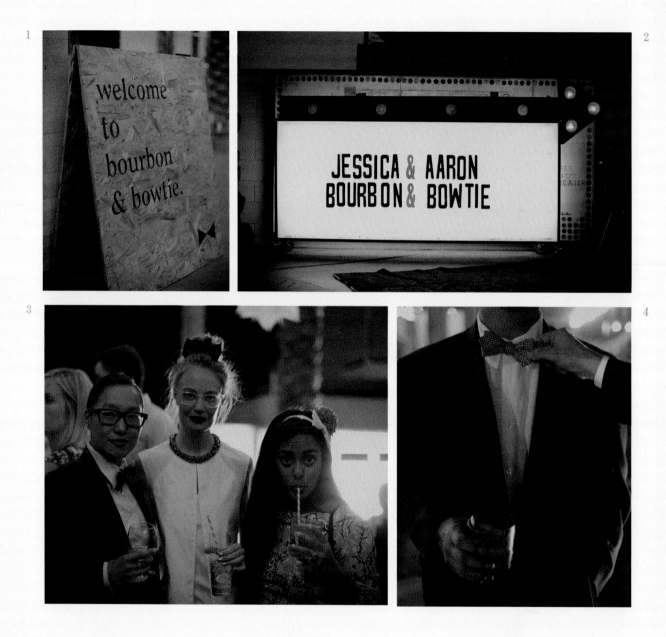

1 GREETINGS
Friends and family were greeted with this short-and-sweet welcome message, which we stenciled onto a composite-wood sandwich board with midnight-blue paint. The bow-tie logo in the bottom right corner was the crowning touch.

2 MARQUEE
An on-site marquee trumpeted the first night's festivities, which centered around a bourbon-themed cocktail party straight out of the Jazz Age.

3, 4 ATTIRE
Retro-inspired glamour was the theme of the night. Guests dressed to impress in sequins, suits, and eye-popping accessories. Gentlemen looked dapper in artisan-crafted bow ties by Forage Haberdashery, gifts from the bride and groom.

If I cannot drink Bourbon and smoke cigars in Heaven than I shall not go.

MARK TWAIN

5 QUOTE CARDS
Cards printed with quotes about bourbon (also designed by Robert and Gary Williams) were scattered around the bar. This one, from Mark Twain, was one of our favorites.

6 MENU
The menu featured an enticing list of bourbon-based cocktails. The most memorable was the ominously titled "Babe's Demise," which paired bacon-infused bourbon with orange and medjool dates.

1

1 ACCESSORIES

LA-based accessory company ban.do
set up shop with a glittering display of
headbands, brooches, and corsages
curated especially for the party.

2 THE BAR

Guests sampled more than ten different
varieties of bourbon throughout the
night and were treated to a selection of
bourbon-themed tapas and desserts.
Bourbon cheesecake, anyone?

3 SETTING

We transformed the Ace's Amigo Room
bar into a modern speakeasy with lots of
warm, rich colors and soothing candlelight.

MENU
Printed menus in polished dark-wood
frames were illuminated on the bar by
a smattering of votive candles.

CHEESES
Partygoers snacked on a medley of
gourmet cheeses, including sharp
cheddar, Gouda, Swiss Gruyère, and
Danish fontina.

COCKTAIL STIRRERS
Not a single detail was overlooked: we
printed hundreds of these wooden cocktail
stirrers with the night's signature logo.

1, 2

1 SETTING

Day two began with Jessica and Aaron's take on a traditional Thai blessing ceremony. For the "blessingmony," a small group of close friends and family traveled with the bride and groom to the desert in Joshua Tree. Guests collected objects from the desert—driftwood, rocks, quartz, plants—to present to the couple as tokens of good luck and best wishes.

2 ATTIRE

Jessica wore a flowing, light-as-air Alexander McQueen dress. To complement her natural look, we fashioned a simple headband out of muslin, globe thistle, and wax flower—just the right match for her wavy, cascading locks.

3 MASTER OF CEREMONY
We created a special garland for the "blessingmony" officiant (a close friend of the couple's) using seeded eucalyptus and desert greens.

4 iT HOUSE
Jessica and Aaron rented Joshua Tree's stunning iT House (an 1,100-square-foot house made of glass) for the ceremony and a post-blessings breakfast gathering. "We loved the contrast between the Ace and the iT House," says Jessica. "The iT House was the perfect place to be contemplative and quiet."

FOOD

1 PASTRIES

Early eaters were greeted with a spread of freshly baked breakfast goods: coffee cake muffins wrapped in tissue paper, buttery maple scones, and miniature loaves of lemon-raspberry bread. The décor was subtle and desert-inspired. Rustic wooden planks and vintage brass goblets filled with desert flora were all we needed.

2 NAPKINS

Aaron's mother made these graphic gray-and-yellow napkins using a patterned fabric designed by Robert and Gary Williams. Afterward, the bride and groom took them home as cherished mementos. "I wanted something I could use every day that would take me back to that morning," says Jessica. "We use those napkins every time we sit down to have a meal."

3 FOOD

Guests who'd worked up an appetite during the ceremony were in for a treat. A build-your-own omelet station, fully loaded with a scrumptious selection of meats, cheeses, vegetables, and herbs, ensured that no one left hungry.

POOL PARTY

1

2

opposite **BEACH BALLS**
These black-and-white beach balls—
which we brought in by the hundreds—
were a hit with everyone. Buoys (pictured
at bottom right) doubled as beer coolers.

1 SMILEBOOTH
Guests posed for playful photos in the
Smilebooth, a modern, do-it-yourself
version of a traditional photo booth.

2 A&J
There was an abundance of both
sunshine and smiles on this crystal-clear
afternoon. (We created this cheery sun
logo using a stencil and yellow chalk.)

3 LEFTOVER CUTIES
Southern California's Leftover Cuties
supplied the party's spunky, nostalgic
soundtrack. We loved the way singer
Shirli McAllen's mustard-colored
dress fit the afternoon's sunny vibe
so seamlessly.

3

DANCE PARTY

1 MENU
The day came to a close with a family-style dinner and a spirited, late-night dance party. The dinner menu featured filet mignon, cold tomato soup, organic cheeses, and a celebratory tequila toast.

2 BALLOONS
Giant Geronimo balloons in pink, orange, yellow, and green were marked with the couple's initials in gold tape.

3 ESCORT CARDS
Guests were welcomed with escort cards fastened to hand-painted feather arrows in glitter-filled glass containers.

4 CENTERPIECES
These stately unicorns stole the show. We bought dozens at a toy store and gave each a coat of glossy gold paint.

5 TABLETOP DÉCOR
Tablescapes were punctuated with brightly colored floral elements—hot-pink boronia, ranunculus, chamomile, craspedia, and solidago—in vintage milk glass vases, metallic mason jars, and bottles in different shades of blue and teal. Table numbers were hand-stenciled in turquoise onto tall glass water jugs. Our motto that night: the more color, the better!

opposite **CHAIRS**

Dinner party seating included Marais, Eames, and hairpin Bentwood chairs dipped in turquoise and ivory paint from Yeah! Rentals. On the day of the party, we started by arranging the 150 chairs symmetrically; then, at the last minute, we switched a few around for a mismatched look, just for fun.

1 SETTING

We made it our mission to create an explosion of color in sunset hues. Festive fabric garlands, vibrant floral elements, and metallic accents complemented the lively atmosphere. "It was a loud, brightly colored, dance-all-night-long kind of vibe," says Jessica. "Really different from the night of the wedding."

2 DANCING

The evening's main event: a raucous dance party under the stars. Instead of the conventional "first dance" on the day of their nuptials, Jessica and Aaron bucked tradition and enjoyed a "last dance" as a nonmarried couple the night before.

3 CONFETTI

Following a round of toasts, cannons showered the dance floor in silver and gold confetti.

DAY 3 | THE WEDDING

1 TYPEWRITER NOTE

The groom left a typewritten note for his bride-to-be on the morning of their wedding. (The love letter wasn't the only surprise—the typewriter itself, a stunning vintage model in fire-engine red, was part of the gift as well.)

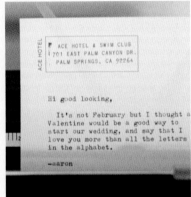

2 DRESS

Jessica's Reem Acra gown featured an elegant T-back and an exquisite beaded neckline. "I wanted something that was right for the vibe of the day," she says. "This dress didn't feel uptight, and that was important to me."

3 SHAVE

Groomsmen received straight-razor shaves courtesy of Rudy's Barbershop in a hotel room–turned–makeshift–salon.

4 SHOT

The bride calmed her wedding-day jitters with a last-minute shot of tequila. "I'm not much of a champagne drinker, to be honest," she admits. "Tequila is my spirit of choice."

2

3

4

1   2   3   4

opposite BRIDE'S BOUQUET
The bride's bouquet was a white-and-cream dream, with heirloom roses, snowberries, seeded eucalyptus, and local wildflowers. "I wanted to avoid anything too flashy, too 'bridal,'" she explains.

1, 2, 3 BRIDESMAIDS' BOUQUETS
We created a variety of monochromatic floral arrangements for Jessica's bridesmaids, using white astrantia, snowberries, and blue thistle. "All of the bridesmaids were wearing white dresses, so we were working with a clean palette," says Jessica. "We wanted everything to feel a little raw and unkempt."

4 BOUTS
Olive-leaf boutonnieres were accented with wax flowers, snowberries, and dried seed pods. Each was tied with a length of braided jute.

1 MARCHING BAND

An hour-long procession led by the Palm Springs High School marching band preceded the ceremony. This was Jessica and Aaron's take on a *baraat*, an Indian wedding tradition in which the groom is brought to the ceremony as part of a parade, surrounded by family and friends. According to custom, the groom often makes his entrance on horseback; for Aaron's arrival, we chose a vintage Jaguar.

2

3

4

2, 3 CEREMONY

The ceremony took place in a rock circle in the Ace's Commune event space. Jessica and Aaron incorporated the tradition of a marriage rug into their vows, standing during the ceremony on a small tapestry brought from home. "Everything was really relaxed," says Jessica. "We had a few benches for people to sit on if they wanted, but otherwise, guests were standing or lying out on the grass. I felt like they enveloped us in a really organic way. It felt like a big hug."

4 EXIT

Guests bid adieu to the happy couple (for a short while, anyway). "We jumped into the car and our friends pushed us out of the venue," remembers the bride. "I like to think of that moment as a metaphor for how our friendships will be for the rest of our lives."

1

2

3

1 SIGN
We love the look of string art. This sandwich board sign (with letters crafted from ivory and pale-pink twine) was so much fun to make.

2 BRASS BAND
The legendary Rebirth Brass Band brought a measure of Big Easy funk to the night's festivities (the nine-piece ensemble was flown in for the occasion, all the way from New Orleans).

4

3 STREET FAIR
We set up a makeshift "street fair" outside the Commune space, with cloth-covered hay bales scattered about as seating.

4 FOOD TRUCKS
Guests were spoiled for choice when it came to cuisine. We lined the street with tantalizing temptations: a taco stand, a hot dog vendor, doughnut fryers, and an ice cream cart. You name it, it was there.

5 KNOCKOUTS
Jessica and Aaron put up their dukes with a treasured set of boxing gloves, a wedding gift from dear friends. "They have a saying: 'It's not about who wins the small battles; it's about winning the long fight,'" says Jessica. "The gloves were a nod to that."

WINE COUNTRY GLAMOUR

ALEXA & MATT

DON'T BE FOOLED. ALEXA AND MATT MAY LOOK LIKE THEY'VE JUST STEPPED OUT OF THE PAGES OF *VOGUE*, BUT IN THE FLESH, THEY'RE GOOD-HUMORED, DOWN-TO-EARTH, AND FULL OF HAPPY SURPRISES.

The ideas they brought to the table were bubbling with contradiction—and we loved it. They wanted to wed the classic elegance of a Sonoma vineyard with design elements that were thoroughly modern. Invitations and paper signage featured a geometric pattern in earthy shades of peach. Pristine flower arrangements shared the stage with bell jars and rock crystals. Guests were served champagne, filet mignon, and chocolate mousse on natural linen tablecloths before taking home small jars of sage honey as party favors. It was a wedding that demonstrated that opposites don't just attract—they're also attractive.

VISION STATEMENT:

Old-fashioned elegance meets geometric hip.
A chic soiree pairing the classic sophistication
of California wine country with a design-
savvy, ultramodern flair.

KEY WORDS:

Polished, earthy, paradoxical.

CHATTER:

Alexa: I love good wine, gourmet food, and
rock crystals. What are your thoughts?

Us: As long as it's not gourmet rock candy,
we're intrigued.

Alexa: I should also mention that Matt is a
music fanatic, and we'll be taking dance
lessons for our first dance.

Us: We fully support that idea. Who wouldn't
want to see the two of you cut a rug? Eye candy
is just the sort of treat we can get behind.

Alexa: You're sweet—no pun intended.
As far as location, we're thinking Sonoma
County. It's close to our home in San Francisco,
and both our families love it. How do you feel
about traveling?

Us: Consider us there.

metal buckets

rock crystals

antique glass

Polish without
pretension:
Alexa and Matt
in a nutshell.

ikat fabric

VALLEY, CALIFORNIA 1909

SAVE THE DATE
alexa & matt
AUGUST 6, 2011

POST CARD

This space for correspondence

This side is for the Address.

On Saturday, August 6th, 2011,

alexa & *matt*
MALOTT   TONNER

are getting married at the
Carneros Inn in Napa, California

Ryan Stem + Tim Barber

San Francisco, CA 94102

Join us for a day of
fun, love, and celebration

PAPER GOODS

opposite SAVE THE DATE

We used a vintage photograph of Sonoma Valley for the couple's postcard-style save-the-date invite. A cheeky detail we're especially fond of: the blush-pink wineglass stain in the bottom left corner. Very appropriate for the setting!

WEDDING PROGRAM

We kept the geometric triangle theme (which we pulled from Alexa and Matt's wedding invitations) consistent through-out the entire day. "I picked out the invitations from Bella Figura, and then Bash, Please used the triangles on the invite as inspiration for the rest of the paper goods, from the programs to the menus," says Alexa.

ATTIRE & BOUQUETS

1

2

1 GROOM'S SUIT

The groom's choice of a slate gray Zegna suit was met with unanimous approval. "Matt's family was in town, and we decided to find him a suit for the wedding," Alexa explains. "After doing some hunting— and with the help of a great salesman at Nordstrom—we found the perfect slim-cut suit. We were all excited to see him in it—he looked great!"

2 DRESS

The bride's show-stopping dress was custom-made from two different Monique Lhuillier gowns. "I knew I didn't want a dress that would overwhelm me with a ton of volume or pouf," she says. "It was a dream dress. It had the most amazing floating quality to it. And I was in love with the keyhole neckline."

3 BRIDAL BOUQUET

Alexa's lush, ultrafeminine bouquet contained cream-colored patience garden roses, trailing passion vine, and, aptly enough, 'Blushing Bride' protea. "I saw a sample of our centerpieces before the wedding, but my bouquet was a complete surprise," says Alexa. "I couldn't have been happier. I couldn't stop staring at it."

4 BRIDESMAIDS' PENDANTS
Before the ceremony, Alexa presented
each of her four bridesmaids with a geode
pendant. "I wanted to thank them with a
gift, and I found these geode necklaces
with the edges dipped in silver on Etsy,"
she says. "The seller, Solis Jewelry, helped
me pick one for each bridesmaid. I gave
them out as we were getting ready."

WEDDING THIS WAY

1 SIGNAGE
Hand-painted signage helped direct guests to the ceremony, with messages like, This Way, Almost There, and Keep Going. Seeded eucalyptus posies dressed up the whitewashed wooden posts.

THE CEREMONY

2

3

2 CEREMONY FLOWERS
As they recited their vows, the bride and groom stood on a carpet of ivory rose petals. Galvanized steel sap buckets holding pineapple mint, oregano, eucalyptus, and local wildflowers formed a beautiful, fragrant "altar."

3, 4, *following spread* **SETTING**
The ceremony took place at the Carneros Inn, a resort in an orchard that overlooks Sonoma Valley. "When we toured the Inn, we fell in love with the views, the layout, and the fig and apple trees planted on the property," says Alexa. "It felt like the perfect place to celebrate."

4

RECEPTION DÉCOR

1

2

1 ESCORT CARDS

In an updated spin on predetermined dinner seating, we compiled table lists, and then guests chose their own seats. We suspended the lists from the branches of a fig tree using strips of frayed cotton linen so they'd twirl with the breeze.

2 PLACE SETTINGS

Menus rested on blue-and-white ikat napkins, which were specially made for the event. For dinner that evening: tomato panzanella, diver scallops with roasted shallots, and a choice of salmon, summer squash risotto, or a classic New York strip steak. Also on hand: a beautiful selection of fine wines with each course—we were in Napa, after all.

3 GARLAND

Paper garlands (featuring the wedding's trademark triangles) were hung from the chairs belonging to the bride and groom. Making them was as easy as pie: we started by dip-dyeing sheets of white paper in various shades of pink and orange, and then we cut them into uniform triangles. A quick trip through a sewing machine, and voilà: party ready.

TABLETOP

1, 2

1 FLORAL CENTERPIECES

Metal buckets filled with a vast assortment of fresh flowers and greenery served as centerpieces. We love simple silver pails for their beauty and versatility—here, they served as unpretentious attendants to our opulent tabletop floral displays.

2 TABLE NUMBERS

We love an element of contrast when it comes to décor. To add a bit of industrial modernism to Alexa and Matt's elegant tablescapes, we used metal home address numbers (which can be found at most hardware stores) to mark tables.

opposite TABLECLOTHS

We often recommend upgrading from standard white tablecloths to custom linens. It's money well spent, since the right cloth adds warmth, texture, and personality. In Alexa and Matt's case, dove-gray linen tablecloths created a clean backdrop for the sweet-smelling, scene-stealing floral arrangements and cloched geodes.

1, 2

3

1 FLOWERS

Floral variety was essential: heirloom roses, olive leaf, seeded eucalyptus, pineapple mint, oregano, silver brunia, white Veronica, ranunculus, scabiosa pods, thistle, local wildflowers, and wheat were all a part of Alexa and Matt's tabletop mix.

2 BOTTLES & BELL JARS

A hodgepodge of inkwells, votive candles, and old medicine bottles—corralled from our favorite flea markets, vintage stores, and Ebay antique sellers—added romance. Bell jars were incorporated to lend a museum feel to the geode display and to underscore the rocks' precious attributes.

3 GEODES

Kyanite crystals, geodes, and salt rock piles were striking additions to the tabletops. Sourced from Ebay and our own private collection, the rocks lent ethereal beauty—and a bit of an earthy edge—to the existing formal spread.

PARTING GIFTS

1 LEAVE YOUR MARK

Guests signed their names on a custom-printed poster that's now framed and on display in the couple's home. To ensure that everyone knew what to do, we created a sign for the table that read: You Were Here. Let Us Hear About It. Leave Your Mark.

2, *opposite* SAGE HONEY JARS

Jars of Hurley Farms sage honey (with labels bearing the couple's names) were stacked on top of wooden wine crates and distributed as party favors at the end of the night. Flowers provided a beautiful, natural backdrop for the display.

CHAPTER
{ № 5 }

SOUTHERN
COOL

RYAN & TIM

WHILE WE WERE INITIALLY DRAWN TO THEIR CHARM AND
POISE, SAN FRANCISCO COUPLE RYAN AND TIM REALLY HAD US
AT "FRIED OKRA." THEY ARE DESIGNERS BY DAY AND EPICURES
BY NIGHT, SO BOTH THE MENU AND THE AESTHETICS OF THEIR
AUSTIN, TEXAS, WEDDING WERE OF EQUAL IMPORTANCE.

To marry Southern comfort with California contemporary, we offset the down-home
feel of the Hotel Saint Cecilia with crisp, chevron-patterned flair. It rained the day of the
wedding, but not even that could dampen the couple's spirits. Ryan simply lifted her train
and soldiered on, proving she's got both the natural grace of a Southern girl and the ef-
fervescent spirit of a true Californian.

VISION STATEMENT:

Southern warmth meets San Francisco cool.
An outdoor shindig under the oak trees
of Austin at the most stylish boutique hotel
in town.

KEY WORDS:

Cheerful, easygoing, food focused.

CHATTER:

Ryan: I'm not the typical bride who has
it all figured out, but I do want something
memorable and unique.

Us: Just like your haircut.

Tim: Isn't she adorable? My pumpkin.

Us: It's clear to see you two are in it for
the long haul. And "pumpkin"? You must
be foodies.

Ryan: You bet. We've got our hearts set
on fried okra. Tomato cocktails, too.

Us: In the coolest city in the South, no less.

Tim: Did we mention we'd like "California
Love" to be our recessional song?

Us: Sounds like the best of both worlds.

striped straws

antique accents

okra

Sunshine-inspired florals brought warmth to Ryan and Tim's rainy day wedding.

chevron print

ATTIRE & BOUQUETS

1 BRIDESMAIDS' BOUQUETS

Ryan's bridesmaids carried cheery yellow-and-white bouquets of Craspedia, Ranunculus, spray roses, and wax flower, offset with clusters of silver brunia. The sunny bursts of yellow (Ryan's favorite color) made the bridesmaids' canary-colored pumps pop.

2 BRIDAL BOUQUET

For Ryan's bouquet, we added a smattering of creamy heirloom roses to the bridesmaids' mix, and bound the arrangement with a cotton grosgrain ribbon. Held against the bodice of her strapless Vera Wang gown, its colors appeared to glow. "I just wanted elegant, simple, and a touch romantic," the bride recalls.

3 GROOMSMEN'S BOUTS

We tied grosgrain ribbon around baby Craspedia, silver brunia, and wax flowers to make the boutonnieres. The colors in these arrangements matched the groomsmen's yellow-and-gray floral bow ties.

4 WRISTLETS

To honor Ryan and Tim's strong connection to family, we fashioned delicate, ribbon-wrapped wristlets for their mothers and grandmothers to wear on the special day. (For continuity's sake, we used the same arrangement as the boutonnieres.)

following spread We wish we could take credit for this dazzling neon "SOUL" sign; alas, it's a poolside fixture at Austin's ultra-hip Hotel Saint Cecilia. "The hotel was an incredible venue," says Ryan. "You don't have to add much for it to feel amazingly special."

SIGNAGE

1 ESCORT CARDS

Typewritten escort tags were wrapped around Craspedia stems and placed in a collection of slender glass bottles.

2 SIGNAGE

We painted these punchy wooden signs to match the yellow flowers displayed on the dining tables. The inspiration for the shape came from the Hotel Saint Cecilia sign: a hanging, neon-lit crest.

3 FLOWERS

Craspedia, wax flower, seeded eucalyptus, garden roses, and white Ranunculus made this bountiful bouquet pop. (And the vintage vessel it's arranged in proved a handy place to prop a sweet-willed reminder.)

TABLESCAPES

opposite TABLE SETTINGS

Black-and-white chevron-print napkins—custom-made, of course—and gleaming gold chargers were the perfect balance of sophistication and fun. (Much like the evening's dinner menu, by AnyStyle Catering, which included fried okra, corn bread with honey butter, and pork tenderloin stuffed with mushroom and kale.)

opposite TABLES & CHAIRS

Guests were seated for dinner family-style at two extra-long dining tables. Snow-white tablecloths and a host of black folding chairs from Marquee Rents helped tie together the evening's color scheme—and matched the design of the napkins perfectly.

PROGRAMS

Printed programs (in the wedding's signature colors) doubled as charming handheld fans—which, as fate and the weather gods would have it, we didn't end up needing. "It rained for the first time in Texas in nine months on our wedding day," Ryan says. "So there was a heightened sense of drama that only rain can bring!"

1, 2

1 TEACUPS

Textured milk glass teacups overflowed with white dahlia, fresh mint, yellow Ranunculus, Craspedia, wax flowers, and exploding grass. Displayed alongside lush ferns in copper pots, these petite arrangements added brightness and charm to the communal-style feasting tables.

2 VINTAGE GLASSWARE

It may be a cliché, but we have to admit that it's absolutely true: there's nothing more romantic than dining by candlelight. For Ryan and Tim's evening meal, dozens of votive candles flickered from inside Moroccan-inspired gold-leaf glasses.

3 PATTERN

The Hotel Saint Cecilia's smart Southern rock aesthetic inspired much of Ryan and Tim's wedding décor. For instance, we chose a chevron print for the napkins—which we sewed ourselves—to match the eye-catching pattern of the hotel lobby floor.

CHAPTER

{ №6 }

URBAN

ORGANIC

KRISTEN & JOHN

IN A PERFECT WORLD, KRISTEN AND JOHN WOULD HAVE TIED THE KNOT IN THE MIDDLE OF NOWHERE, BAREFOOT ON THE SANDS OF A REMOTE BEACH OR A DESERT ISLAND, SUR-ROUNDED BY AN INTIMATE GROUP OF FAMILY AND FRIENDS.

In reality, a city wedding proved more sensible—so we brought the great outdoors to them. Working off the austere décor of L.A.'s magnificent Marvimon loft, we gathered cactus wood and cattails, filled mason jar candleholders with sand, and constructed the bride's bouquet using wheat and balsa. Everyone pitched in. Kristen and John built their own *chuppah* out of burlap and bamboo, the bridesmaids strung gypsy-inspired garlands, and as an extra-special touch, we fashioned a Just Hitched sign out of jute and wire to hang from the couple's dinner chairs.

VISION STATEMENT:

Backyard candlelight meets big-city sparkle.
A warmhearted wedding featuring a
harmonious medley of all-natural textures
and time-honored, tasteful touches.

KEY WORDS:

Wild, woodsy, communal.

CHATTER:

Kristen: My mom wants a storybook romance
and lots of lace. I want a secluded beach and
boatloads of burlap.

Us: Let's come up with a compromise.
We'll bring in cotton, linen, wheat, and sand,
plus lots of candles and farm-fresh food.
And to balance rugged with refined, we'll trim
the burlap you love with lace.

Kristen: That sounds enchanting.

Us: We think so, too. Let's talk basics.
What's your favorite color?

Kristen: Earthy.

Us: Interesting. We'd love to hear more.

Kristen: You know: wood, grass, sand, rust.
I want everyone at the wedding to feel
connected to the earth.

Us: You got it. Let's get dirty.

copper vessels

hand-sewn flowers

natural twine

organic fabrics and lace

Kristen and John challenged us to bring elements of the outdoors in.

ATTIRE & BOUQUETS

1
2

3

1 GROOM'S SUIT

J. Crew's classic gray Ludlow suit was a perfect fit (literally) for the groom. "John wanted the process of suit shopping to be as pain-free as possible," says Kristen. "We went to the store, he put this one on—and it fit beautifully. We didn't even have to get it altered. It was effortless."

2 BRIDAL DRESS

After weeks of searching for the perfect dress, Kristen stumbled upon an unlikely candidate among a selection of ready-to-wear items at Monique Lhuillier. "It was a maroon cocktail dress," she says, "and I ended up collaborating with them to modify it. We changed the color to off-white and removed the original halter top for an understated, Grecian-inspired look."

3 GOLD SHOES

Though she originally planned to wear flip-flops, Kristen couldn't resist these gleaming gold pumps from Kate Spade.

4, 5 BRIDAL BOUQUET

Kristen's dry bouquet contained wheat, scabiosa pods, balsa-wood flowers, and oregano. We finished the arrangement with fresh magnolia leaves and a natural braided ribbon. "It was perfect," she says. "I cried when I saw it." Prior to the big day, Kristen put together a mock-up of John's boutonniere for us to use as inspiration. The final version was made using a simple, carved-wood flower.

WELCOME TABLE

1

opposite PUMPKINS
White pumpkins in a variety of shapes and sizes were an arresting (and unusual) accent to the tabletop.

opposite TABLECLOTH
Wedding favors, framed photographs of the couple, and nature-inspired décor rested atop a vintage crewel tablecloth, a beautiful find from L.A.'s Rose Bowl Flea Market. "We wanted to balance coarse, textured fabrics with delicate materials," says the bride, "for just a hint of sweetness."

1 FABRIC GARLAND
"For my bachelorette party," says Kristen, "I had my girlfriends go to a fabric store and bring back fun materials. We used the swatches to make the garlands that hung above our welcome table."

2 FABRIC FLOWERS
Craft guru Ashley Meaders stitched linen and muslin flowers of various sizes to use as decorative accents. We sprinkled them over tabletops and pinned them to the sides of the seating chart board.

2

1 POSTCARDS

In a unique play on a guest book, we stacked an assortment of graphic postcards (purchased from Anthropologie) in a wooden box, along with a jar of colored pencils carved from twigs, and instructions for guests to sign a message for the bride and groom.

2 MATCH BOXES

These commemorative matchbooks featured the couple's initials and an equine logo in palest green. "John had just gone on a trip to Wyoming and had fallen in love with the horses there. We have a dream of having our own one day," Kristen says. "Also, John calls me Pony, so it was the perfect choice."

3 SEED BOMBS

Kristen is a nature lover with a passion for gardening and wildflowers. We paid homage to her love of the outdoors with Commonstudio seed bombs as wedding favors. (We packaged the seeds in gocco-printed canvas drawstring bags.) "Since we compromised on having our wedding downtown, it was important to us for nature to be present," says Kristen.

please take a
seed bomb
& spread the world
with wildflowers in
celebration of love.

TABLESCAPES

1

2

opposite **TABLETOP DÉCOR**
Rustic and earthy, Kristen and John's table-top décor reinforced the night's back-to-nature theme. Marvimon's mounted goat bust presided over the festivities.

1 MENUS
Menus were printed on kraft paper and displayed on miniature clipboards. Rack of lamb, bone-in branzino, and Heirloom LA's much-loved "lasagna cupcakes" were among the delicacies served. "Our tasting at Heirloom blew us away," says Kristen.

2 TABLE MARKERS
The bride loves to garden, so many of the materials for the tabletop décor came from a local gardening shop. To start, we tucked circular kraft paper table numbers into copper mugs filled with soft moss. Then, for the bride and groom's place settings, we laid metal garden stakes—wrapped in twine and marked with their initials—on top of their dinner plates.

1, 2

1 FLOWERS

For the tabletops, we gathered a woodsy
mix of floral elements: succulents,
balsa wood, yellow kangaroo paw, wheat,
twigs, dahlia, and oregano.

2 STENCIL BOXES

Centerpieces were arranged inside
rectangular wooden planting boxes.
To personalize them for the evening,
we stenciled celebratory words, such
as *love*, *enjoy*, *yes*, and *splendor* in
script (the font, Buttermilk, was created
by designer Jessica Hische).

3 ROMANTIC MESSAGES

A gift from the groom to his bride,
these sweet paintings—there were four
total—featured phrases borrowed from
one of Kristen's childhood report cards.
"I was so moved," she says.

PRAISE
EFFORTS

SENSITIVE
TO HER
NEEDS

4 CANDLES WITH SAND
To bring a bit of the beach to the big city, we filled mason jars and hurricane candle holders with sand and white votives, and then tied textured rope around the rims.

following spread **JUST HITCHED**
This one-of-a-kind, handmade embellishment was one of our favorite details from the day. We wrapped wire in twine and used it to shape the script lettering and hung the finished sign from the bride's and groom's dining chairs with frilly white ribbon.

DESSERT TABLE

1

2

1, 3 APPLE PIE POPS

Apple pie pops from Sweet and Saucy Shop were just one of many mouthwatering goodies on display that night. Also up for grabs: inside-out s'mores, oatmeal cream pies, and peanut butter cakewiches, all provided by the ever-reliable Cake Monkey.

2 CAKE

"A big wedding cake wasn't a priority for us," says Kristen. Instead, this chocolate confection from Cake Monkey did the trick. The wire toppers were made by the bride herself. "I wanted to add a special touch," she says.

EUROPEAN DESERT

BETH & GEOFF

SUBSTITUTING LOS ANGELES FOR THE ARIZONA DESERT, BETH AND GEOFF'S CEREMONY RADIATED ROMANCE. A MIX OF RUSTS, ORANGES, SOFT PEACHES, AND MOSSY GREENS CONTRIBUTED TO AN ORGANIC COLOR PALETTE.

Vintage mercury glasses filled with succulents, heirloom roses, thistle, and wild wheat commingled with perfectly patined garden pots and wood stumps resting atop moss beds. The menu boasted a variety of homemade pastas, reflecting Beth and Geoff's shared love of Italian culture and cuisine—the couple even included silver pasta-shaped key chains (courtesy of the bride's stepfather) as wedding favors. In the end, the sunset made for a brilliant hot-pink sky, and guests danced in the desert air until the wee hours. If only for a moment, we could have sworn we were in Tuscany.

VISION STATEMENT:

Italian intrigue meets the Arizona desert. An invigorating, back-to-nature event balancing well-mannered grace with natural rusticity.

KEY WORDS:

Lush, desert, woodland.

CHATTER:

Beth: Question: Do you guys think a woodland forest setup at an Arizona country club would be out of line?

Us: Absolutely not. We love the idea.

Beth: I'd also like to incorporate a bit of Europe into the night. There's a heavy Italian influence in our home, so I'd love to commemorate that.

Us: Pasta dinner, coming right up.

Beth: I'm so glad you don't think I'm a crazy bride with my oddball ideas.

Us: You're in good hands. Eclectic mash-ups are our specialty.

desert flora

Italian eats

succulent décor

Scottsdale's Silver-
leaf Country Club
set the stage for
Beth and Geoff's
desert-inspired fete.

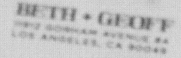
BETH + GEOFF
1182 GORMAN AVENUE #4
LOS ANGELES, CA 90049

TOGETHER WITH THEIR FAMILIES

Beth Whitaker & Geoff Tranchina

REQUEST THE PLEASURE OF YOUR COMPANY AT THEIR WEDDING

Saturday the nineteenth of November
two thousand and eleven
at five o'clock in the evening

Silverleaf Club • Scottsdale, Arizona

DINNER & DELIGHTS TO FOLLOW

+ GEOFF
AM AVENUE #4
ES, CA 90049

KINDLY REPLY BY:
OCTOBER 15, 2011

WHO: _____

—— WOULDN'T MISS IT FOR THE WORLD
—— WILL BE THERE IN SPIRIT
—— NUMBER ATTENDING

INVITATIONS

opposite

WEDDING INVITATIONS

In keeping with their unpolished, outdoor aesthetic, we chose chipboard (enlivened with bright red lettering) for Beth and Geoff's wedding invitations. "The process of planning our paper goods was easy and wonderful," says the bride. "The design on our invitations was based off of some mercury glass containers that I bought at an antiques store." (The containers were later used in the wedding for floral displays.)

REHEARSAL DINNER INVITATIONS

The couple's rehearsal dinner invites were decidedly less formal. We selected a festive image from the vintage postcard website Card Cow, and we did the rest, adding decorative wording and a red, green, and yellow festive flag banner illustration to match the evening's Mexican-themed meal.

LET'S CELEBRATE!

YOU'RE INVITED

P ∘ L ∘ E ∘ A ∘ S ∘ E
JOIN US TO SERENADE
BETH & GEOFF
AT THEIR REHEARSAL DINNER
November 18, 2011
∘ 6 o'clock in the evening ∘
SUSAN & BILL'S HOUSE

deliver to:

ATTIRE & BOUQUETS

1

2

1 BRIDAL BOUQUET

Beth's bouquet was a romantic desert mix of white Ranunculus, succulents, seeded eucalyptus, peach spray roses, Hypericum berries, and white thistle, finished with a green velvet ribbon. (We loved the juxtaposition of the robust desert greens with the softer pink-and-white florals.) "I wanted the flowers to have a rustic feel," says the bride. "I especially love succulents and ranunculus, so it was important for those to be incorporated into the arrangements."

2 BRIDESMAIDS' BOUQUETS

Beth's seven bridesmaids carried bouquets made of silver brunia, white thistle, Ranunculus, and wild desert florals to complement their cream-colored dresses. "I always knew I wanted my bridesmaids to wear different dresses," says Beth. "I think it looks so pretty in pictures, and it makes everyone look happier—each dress fits the person's body the way she wants. The color was a little harder to decide, though. In the end, I thought cream would be easy and beautiful. It fit the look and feel of our wedding."

3 DRESS

"I found my wedding dress at Pebbles Bridal in Woodland Hills," says Beth. "I knew I wanted something simple, with lace, something that had a vintage feel to it. I tried this one on and took it home that day."

4 BOUTS

Boutonnieres were constructed for Geoff and his attendants using an assortment of wild desert greens. We tied each by hand with soft velvet ribbon. The groom wore his on the lapel of a Joseph Abboud tuxedo. "When I first saw Geoff on the day of the wedding, I thought he looked amazing," Beth says. "But also a little nervous!"

CHUPPAH FLOWERS

CHUPPAH FLOWERS

Beth and Geoff's *chuppah* was draped in gauzy white linen and bedecked with a spray of white and ivory garden roses, lotus pods, golden amaranthus, seeded eucalyptus, thistle, and Queen Anne's lace. We assembled the florals on-site the morning of the wedding, drawing inspiration from the stunning beauty of the surrounding landscape. Fresh air, majestic mountains, a seemingly boundless sky—we kept having to pause to take it all in. We thought the arrangement turned out beautifully, but most importantly, so did our bride and groom—and their friends and family, too. "I loved the *chuppah*'s simplicity and all of the beautiful flowers attached," says Beth. "Many of our guests complimented its design."

FAVORS

2

1 PASTA KEY RING FAVORS

"My husband is part Italian, and we love pasta," says Beth. "My stepfather, a jeweler, made key chain molds from real pasta noodles—fusilli, bow tie, and penne. Then he cast them in silver."

2 BREAD TIN ESCORT CARDS

Beth found these vintage metal bread tins while shopping at a flea market prior to the wedding. The day of the ceremony, we filled them with moss and used them to display escort cards that had been calligraphed by the bride's aunt.

3 MAD LIBS

Beth and Geoff's guest book was a witty play on the childhood word game Mad Libs. Guests filled in descriptive terms about the couple and their future together.

3

TABLETOP FLOWERS

1

2

3

1 FLOWERS

To accentuate the dining tables, we cushioned polished wooden boxes on beds of moss, and filled them with an organic mix of brown Amaranthus, seeded eucalyptus, white garden roses, peach spray roses, wild desert greens, lotus pods, thistle, and succulents.

2 WOODEN FLOWERS

Beth ordered dozens of these tiny decorative flowers from the Etsy shop Accents and Petals. Made from wood chips, they served as the perfect centerpieces for her sand-hued napkins.

3 SUCCULENTS

Potted succulents were a rustic counterpoint to the soft tabletop floral arrangements.

4 VASES

We used an assortment of tiny vintage bottles from our own in-office collection to hold pale pink single-stem roses.

CHAPTER

{ №8 }

GARDEN
PARTY

SARAH & MICHAEL

SARAH AND MICHAEL ARE TWO EXTREMELY BUSY ENTREPRE-
NEURS (THEY'RE AT THE HELM OF THE POPULAR SALON CHAIN
DRYBAR), SO THEY TURNED THE WEDDING-PLANNING REINS
OVER TO US COMPLETELY. THIS MEANT MINIMAL CONSULTA-
TION AND HEAPS OF TRUST—UNHEARD OF IN THIS BUSINESS.

Ultimately, we brought lots of imagination (and a pinch of tradition) to their Brentwood
backyard wedding, which featured a dance party in an art studio located behind the house.
With the freedom of a blank canvas, we painted words and graphics on the studio wall, including the bride's favorite e. e. cummings poem. Even the ceiling got a makeover: we draped
the raw beams with linen and, as a finishing touch, hung a rotating disco ball. Party time.

VISION STATEMENT:

Backyard fresh meets dance-floor finesse.
An atypical production, equal parts classic
and current.

KEY WORDS:

Summery, innovative, fresh.

CHATTER:

Sarah: We love what you gals do, and we don't
have time to be involved in design meetings—so
take it and run with it.

Us: We're excited. What is most important to
you about your wedding?

Michael: We want it to be unique—unlike any
other we've seen.

Sarah: I'd love a really fun dance party. And it's
important that the food is outstanding.

Us: You're speaking our language. Can you give
us any colors, themes, or ideas that pop into your
mind when you envision the day?

Sarah: Pinks. Greens. Sparkle and shine.

Michael: Lots of flowers—wildflowers, garden
flowers. Flowers everywhere.

Sarah: I'd like to incorporate my favorite
love poem somehow, but I'll leave the details
up to you.

Us: Not a problem. We'll make sure it sparkles
and shines.

paper chains

rustic platters

disco dancing

E. E. Cummings
SELECTED POEMS

love poems

Luxurious florals stole the spotlight at Sarah and Michael's celebration.

ATTIRE & BOUQUETS

1

2

1 BRIDAL BOUQUET

Assembled by our friends at Los Angeles floral company Dandelion Ranch, Sarah's bouquet was an ultrafeminine blend of café au lait dahlias, garden roses, and Dusty Millers. The bride, who requested a "lush and unique" arrangement of peaches, creams, sage, and lime green, wanted the floral elements in her bouquet to echo those on the *chuppah*.

2 BRIDESMAIDS' ATTIRE

Sarah's bridesmaids accessorized neutral J. Crew dresses with glittered TOMS shoes and oversized jeweled necklaces from Madewell. "I thought those would make for nice, unique bridesmaids' gifts," says Sarah. Their bouquets—made up of a variety of multi-colored roses— "complemented the dresses and the whole space in general," she adds.

3 DRESS

"I found my dress at One Night Affair in L.A.," says Sarah. "It was by Vera Wang and had delicate, off-the-shoulder sleeves and a giant train. It was so timeless, elegant, and *me*, but at the same time, it was a little unexpected—everyone who knew me assumed I would go with something sleek and simple. I loved the element of glamour and surprise it brought to our front yard nuptials."

4, 5 GROOM'S ATTIRE
For the big day, Michael paired a dashing
gray suit from J. Crew with sneakers.
"The suit was perfect for our wedding,"
says Sarah. "Not too formal, and light-
colored in case the sun was beating
down. And I've always thought he looked
adorable in vests—when I saw him,
I thought, 'That's my handsome husband.'"

A PRIVATE CELEBRATION

The couple was married at a friend's private home in Brentwood, California, under a spectacular garden floral *chuppah* created by Dandelion Ranch. "The wedding was about bringing our family and closest friends together, and what better place to do that than the home of a friend?" says Sarah. "I loved how many different spaces there were for guests to gather over the course of the night. We hugged in tight on the front lawn for the ceremony; gathered for cocktails and live music on the deck; and danced in the backyard studio, which they had painted and decorated exclusively for the wedding. We are so fortunate to have friends who were generous with their home and gave us the gift of the greatest venue imaginable. It was intimate, comfortable, and completely customized for our day."

following spread

WINE CRATE FLOWERS

Sarah and Michael share a passion for travel and good wine (in fact, Sarah is a sommelier). To honor their interests, we displayed floral arrangements by Dandelion Ranch amid a collection of wooden wine crates. A vintage suitcase with emerald-green lining held wedding programs.

BEVERAGE MENU

COCKTAILS

St. Germain Cocktail
elderflower, sauvignon blanc, soda

Dark & Stormier
ginger beer, domaine de canton,
dark rum, lime juice

Summer Watermelon
watermelon vodka, fresh cucumber
juice, splash of simple syrup, lime

Mucho Margarita
classic rocks margarita

The Married Martini
rangtang vodka, white cranberry,
muddled strawberries

BEER
Heineken
Corona

WHITE WINE
Chateau des Cleons
Picton Bay Sauvignon Blanc

RED WINE
La Loggia
Barbera d'alba
Trentare 33 rosso

BUBBLY
Cortisano Cava

Also: Ginger Ale, Tea, Sparkling Water, Cola

SIGNAGE

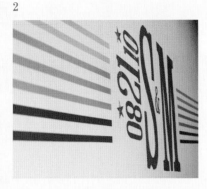

1 BAR MENU

Incorporating Sarah and Michael's favorite summery colors into the design of their paper goods was key. The bar menu, showcased in an unfinished wood frame, featured festive script and a host of happy stripes. (Cocktails, including a "Married Martini" and a "Dark and Stormier," were handcrafted by a local mixologist.)

2 PAINTED DETAILS

The backyard studio's stark white walls cried out for color—and we answered with paintbrushes. Punchy stripes were a given, but the real cherry on top was the e. e. cummings poem "I carry your heart with me," which we hand-stenciled onto the wall for dramatic effect.

3 PROGRAM

The event's trademark stripes were also featured on the programs. "When the bride and groom kiss, high-five your neighbor in honor of Sarah!" the programs read, in reference to one of Sarah's most endearing habits.

1

love chain

1 PAPER CHAIN GUEST BOOK
"We didn't have a guest book," says Sarah.
"Just a paper love chain at the end of the
night, made with notes that our guests
had written." To facilitate the paper-chain
making, we displayed materials—including
strips of paper in a variety of colors—in a
vintage hardware store container that had
originally held address numbers.

2 LOVE CHAIN PHOTO BOOTH
Adding to the paper-chain motif, we
used long strands of green, pink, cream,
and floral-print paper to decorate the
wedding photo booth. The garlands were
fastened to a wooden backdrop we had
painted ourselves.

TABLETOP FLOWERS

opposite CANNING JARS

Single-stem roses rested in canning jars accented with twine, providing visual contrast to the evening's fuller, more elaborate arrangements. Tiny votives with matching ties made inviting, graceful—and decidedly non-frilly—accompaniments.

FLORAL BOXES

At mealtime, we let Dandelion Ranch's lavish florals take center stage, leaving the rest of the tabletop décor clean and understated. Sensuous clusters of café au lait dahlias, garden roses, geraniums, Dusty Millers, and succulents shone in muted wooden boxes. In shades of pink, peach, yellow, and green, they weren't your typical tabletop arrangements—and we loved that.

DESSERT TABLE

1

2

1 PLATTERS

The tree-stump platters were sourced locally from a craft store. We covered them with parchment paper and trimmed them with succulents before assembling these decadent spreads of cake pops.

2, 3 CAKE

"My husband loves cake pops," says Sarah, "and I love him, so this was an easy decision!" Sweet and Saucy Shop provided espresso and double-chocolate cake pops to satisfy the groom's cravings. The couple's Sweet and Saucy Shop wedding cake was a study in stripped-down elegance. "I thought it looked so natural, and it fit right in with the backyard venue," says Sarah.

following spread DISCO BALL

We're firm believers that no dance party is complete without a disco ball. For Sarah and Michael's night, we hung burlap streamers from the studio ceiling to supplement the sparkle.

NOUVEAU CARNIVAL

NINA & AMIR

BOTH ACTORS AND COMEDIANS, NINA AND AMIR SHARE A MU-
TUAL LOVE FOR DRAMA—IN THE BEST POSSIBLE SENSE, OF
COURSE. SO WHEN IT CAME TO THEIR WEDDING, WHICH TOOK
PLACE AT L.A.'S ECO-FRIENDLY MARRAKESH HOUSE, WE TOOK
ALL THE ELEMENTS OF A TRADITIONAL WEDDING AND SPUN
THEM INTO A QUIRKY, KALEIDOSCOPIC CARNIVAL OF SORTS.

The reception featured a modern interpretation of a Persian Sofreh. A gospel choir. A
hookah lounge. A fortune-teller. Comedians dressed in drag. And color? We had it covered. Eye-popping rainbow hues against a clean, black-and-white backdrop set the tone for
a night of merriment—and, of course, laughter.

VISION STATEMENT:

French-Moroccan allure meets comedic charisma. A fanciful, no-holds-barred wedding with a Hollywood twist—and a healthy dose of humor.

KEY WORDS:

Dynamic, colorful, eco-friendly.

CHATTER:

Nina: I want over-the-top color. But no red. I hate red.

Amir: Also, organic food is a must.

Nina: And my mom and I are dancing to "Brick House," no questions asked. And there will be drag queens.

Us: We're glad you guys put so much thought into this already. We can tell you have opinions.

Nina: Oh, I have opinions. Have you seen my stand-up comedy?

Us: We'll YouTube it as soon as we get back to the office.

Nina: What do you think of a black-and-white checkered dance floor?

Amir: A hookah lounge?

Nina: A salted caramel dessert?

Us: Whatever strikes your fancy. Your wish is our command.

a classy canine

candy-colored cake pops

tarot cards

black & white stripes

Nina and Amir requested
color, color, and more
color. We were more than
happy to deliver.

1

FLOWERS

2

1 BRIDAL BOUQUET

Nina's bouquet was an ombre mix of blooms in every color of the rainbow. "I'm not a girly girl," she explains. "I knew I didn't want pastels or whites, or anything subtle or muted. I wanted the flowers to really pop." To accommodate her vision, we put together a vibrant bouquet that included green Lisianthus, fresh mint, pincushion Protea, soft pink peonies, blue thistle, and purple clover.

2 BOUTS

We decided to give the groom a choice of colors to wear throughout the night, so we created five boutonnieres designed to suit any mood. There was a fuchsia option made using pink Nerine; a purple arrangement featuring clover; a yellow cluster of Craspedia and yarrow; an orange option made from tangerine spray roses; and, finally, a lime-colored arrangement of bright-green Ranunculus.

UNIQUE DETAILS

1

1 FLAGS

The wedding took place at Culver City's
Marrakesh House, beloved by the couple
for its beauty and eco-friendly philosophy.
"It's green in a way that's not obtrusive,"
says Amir. "You don't get the sense that it's
a recycled place. It's just a really beautiful
home with a lot of green elements just
underneath the surface." We printed these
muslin ceremony flags with custom stamps
bearing the couple's favorite sayings and
passed them out for guests to wave as the
two exchanged vows.

2

2 HEART RUG
We painted a hot-pink heart on a white rug for the couple to stand on during the ceremony.

3 FORTUNE-TELLING
Guests wishing to have their fortunes told had access to both a palm reader and a tarot card specialist. "I thought it would be a fun thing for people to do if they needed to take a break from dancing," says Nina. We made lawn signs to designate the stations (the palm reader was in a beautiful, Moroccan-style atrium), finishing each with bright, multicolored stripes.

1 SOFREH

The stand-out detail of Amir and Nina's celebration: a modernized Persian Sofreh Aghd. (Traditionally, a Sofreh is a spread of symbolic items common at Persian weddings.) "We wanted not only to modernize the Sofreh, but to really make it personal," says Amir.

2 ORANGE LANTERNS

Tangerine-colored Moroccan lanterns symbolized fire and energy. "We still have them on our mantel," say the couple.

3 SWEETS

A Sofreh commonly includes an assortment of sweets and pastries. Since Nina is from Philadelphia, we supplied soft pretzels and Tastykakes as sentimental details.

1

1 GUEST BOOK

A principal element of a traditional Sofreh is a holy book. "Because neither of us has ever read an entire holy book," Nina and Amir explained on their welcome poster, "we've decided instead to use a book containing the blessings of our friends and family."

2 SOFREH DETAIL

In a traditional Sofreh, Wild Rue seeds (also known as esphand) are present to ward off the evil eye. For Nina and Amir's Sofreh, the groom's mother found esphand to match the wedding's vibrant color palette.

3 PROGRAM DISPLAY

A large welcome poster displayed at the entrance of the Marrakesh House featured an explanation of the Sofreh, a copy of the evening's Heirloom LA menu, and a colorful, playful riff on both the couple's nicknames for one another ("Boo") and the Persian word for kiss ("boose"). "I loved that it was lyrical, poetic, quirky, and fun," says Amir.

3

TABLETOP

1

opposite **TABLE NUMBERS**
Table numbers were drawn with a white paint pen on jet-black wooden tiles, which we propped against each color-themed floral centerpiece. Hand-numbering was done by Los Angeles calligrapher Plurabelle.

1 SEATING CHART
To make Nina and Amir's seating chart, we pinned printed table rosters to wooden boards covered in black-and-white striped fabric. (We chose black-and-white stripes as a clean, consistent backdrop for the night's many eye-popping colors.) Utilizing large boards like this one—and the welcome chart that greeted guests upon their arrival—allowed us to cut down on paper usage, a priority for our eco-conscious bride and groom.

2 FLOWER BOXES
Black wooden planters were heaped with a prismatic array of flowers. This vivid centerpiece featured green Ranunculus, mint, green Lisanthus, blue thistle, purple clover, pink Nerine, orange Ranunculus, yarrow, and Craspedia. Tidy, well-groomed clusters ensured that the rainbow hues remained playful without being clownish.

2

COLORED FLORAL ARRANGEMENTS

Each dining table was assigned a color and accented accordingly with mono-chromatic arrangements in glossy black bowls. "I just wanted lots of color," says Nina. "I wanted the arrangements to be bright and fun."

1 ORANGE

A glowing assortment of Dahlia, Ranunculus, and Celiosa set the orange table ablaze.

2 GREEN

An electric mix of mint, carnations, Lisianthus, spider mums, and Ranunculus brought energy and intensity to the green table.

3 YELLOW

The yellow table was lit with pin cushion Protea, mums, yarrow, Craspedia, and canary-colored carnations.

4 VIOLET

Scabiosa flowers, blue thistle, purple carnations, and clover made for a brilliant, blue-violet centerpiece.

1 2

3 4

1 STRAWS AND STIR STICKS
Black-and-white straws and cocktail
stir sticks were displayed in glass containers tied with pink tulle. We created
the stir sticks using wooden dowels
and Washi tape.

2 SPARKLERS
We loaded sparklers into white mason
jars for guests to light up the dance floor.

3 MATCHBOXES
Matchboxes featuring the couple's
names and the phrase "Bing bong,"
one of their favorite sayings, were
handed out as party favors.

4 BUTTONS
Guests found specially made buttons
(which read "BOO BOOS BOOSE
BOOSES") on their dinner plates.

5 NAPKINS
Cocktail napkins were customized
using a font we designed in the evening's
signature pink.

SWEETS TABLE

SWEETS TABLE

"Neither of us are big fans of wedding cake," says Amir. "We love so many different kinds of desserts, and we love variety. We thought, what if we have twelve different desserts instead? That decision allowed us to play and get creative, and our guests just went crazy for everything. We were able to have cake pops and cupcakes and miniature banana cream pies and *macarons*—so many different tastes and types." In addition to a variety of sweets from Sweet and Saucy Shop, there were tastes of home, as well: Nina baked her husband's favorite oatmeal cookies, and the groom's mother supplied homemade baklava. "We couldn't stop our guests from eating the desserts before it was dessert time," says Amir. "In fact, Nina and I didn't even get to have any!"

COMMUNAL
AFFAIR

ALEXANDRA & GREG

ALEXANDRA AND GREG WERE MARRIED AT A PRIVATE HOME IN THE HIP LOS ANGELES NEIGHBORHOOD LOS FELIZ. A PLEASURE TO WORK WITH, THEY WERE OPEN TO IDEAS AND REMARKABLY THOUGHTFUL IN THEIR PLANNING.

Among the ideas we cooked up together: a ribbon-and-succulents installation to hang from the tree that sheltered them during their exchange of vows; napkins made from patterned fabric designed by the bride, a textile designer; and table numbers crafted from wire jute. As a surprise, we hand-painted a canvas curtain with the couple's names and hung it behind the dinner buffet. Charming, graceful, and artistic—just like the couple themselves.

VISION STATEMENT:

Simple and sweet meets East L.A. chic. A close-knit family affair full of heartfelt— and highly personal—details.

KEY WORDS:

Sweet, graceful, succulents galore.

REVISED DIALOGUE:

Alexandra: I adore succulents. Succulents are a must.

Us: Potted or in terraria?

Alexandra: Whichever holds the most.

Us: Beautiful. We're such fans of your work. Will you design a few textile patterns we can use in the décor?

Alexandra: Of course! Overall, I want the wedding to feel modern and fresh, with details and textures that nod to the California lifestyle.

Us: Right on. Can we be guests?

Alexandra: Please! Come dance the night away with us.

Us: There's nothing we'd love more.

graphic buttons

embellished paper goods

Alexandra

& Greg

August 7, 2010

custom textiles

Paints, stencils, needle and
thread: Alexandra and Greg's
artistic sensibilities inspired
us to get creative.

ATTIRE & BOUQUETS

1

1 DRESS

"I knew I wanted a vintage dress," says the bride. "I found this one at The Way We Wore. I loved the creamy color, the unusual embroidery, and the rhinestone detail. It made me feel timeless." Her husband-to-be agreed: "As I watched Alexandra walk down from the upper garden to the ceremony, there was a row of cypress trees along the pathway that was causing her to disappear and reappear as she walked. The way the sunlight captured her between each tree created an illusion that she was glowing and floating toward me in her dress. It was just beautiful."

2 BRIDAL BOUQUET

Alexandra's bouquet contained pin-cushion Protea, kangaroo paw, orange Dahlias, and succulents, and was tied with a fabric designed by the bride. "When I was asked about the color palette for the flowers," says Alexandra, "I knew I wanted orange and green tones—my favorite combination."

3 BOUTS

We used succulents—the bride's favorite—to make the boutonnieres. (We crafted a simple succulent hairpiece for Alexandra to match.)

1 HANGING FABRIC STREAMERS

Alexandra's patterned textiles provided the perfect materials to make this festive, multicolored bunting. "Incorporating my textile designs into the details gave the décor a unified theme," says the bride. "The printed napkins and the fabric bunting had a unique and meaningful look."

2, *opposite* HANGING SUCCULENT DECORATIONS

We created this hanging installation using glass orbs from CB2, as well as a collection of ribbons and strips from Alexandra's textiles. "After dark, the terraria lit up using LED lights that had been placed in each one," says Alexandra. "It was magical."

SIGNAGE

1 CEREMONY SIGN

Reclaimed wood sourced from a salvage yard downtown was the foundation for this handsome sign; for the lettering, we used a stencil made from the same font as the invitation suite. "Our ceremony was informal and brief, but very personal," remembers the bride. "Our officiant, Jennifer Berry, acknowledged our family and friends, and my 97-year-old grandmother, who gave us her wedding bands. Greg and I shared our vows, filled with emotion and love for one another. We were both very present—we were soaking up each moment. There was so much love between us and our family and friends."

2 MONOGRAMMED SIGN

We hand-painted this cheerful wooden welcome sign and used ivory grosgrain ribbon to tie it to the front gate of the wedding venue (which also happened to be the home of Greg's brother and sister-in-law). "It's a beautiful 1920s home in the foothills of Los Feliz," says Alexandra. "Their terraced garden offered the ideal setting for each phase of the wedding. Greg and I even had a private 'reveal' at the very top of a patio overlooking the hills of Griffith Park."

2

EASEL

Getting to know our clients—and coming up with ways to commemorate their passions and personalities—is one of the most rewarding aspects of our job. (By the time a wedding is over, we often know more about a couple than we do about some of our closest friends.) In Alexandra and Greg's case, we paid tribute to the bride's love of painting by displaying table charts on an old, paint-splattered easel, borrowed for the day from a local artist. We pinned the lists—trimmed with strips of the bride's fabrics—atop a linen-covered wooden board. "My background is in painting and I grew up using an easel," Alexandra says. "I thought this was brilliant."

following spread

SEATING MONOGRAMS

We marked the bride and groom's seats at the table with custom-painted wooden signs, made from scratch. We cut the slabs of wood by hand, stenciled the couple's initials in script, and added a succulent-inspired embellishment below in alternating shades of green. "The dinner was about relishing time with our guests, enjoying the special toasts from our family, and taking the opportunity to mingle," says Alexandra. "The catering by Heirloom was a big hit, too."

TABLETOP

1 SETTING

Alexandra and Greg's guests dined
in the house's cozy interior courtyard,
which featured a romantic outdoor
fireplace and a fountain. Tables were
set with cream cotton linen and topped
with glass bowls filled with succulents.

2, 3, 4 NAPKINS

We used Alexandra's textiles to sew dinner
table napkins. Tiny buttons, fastened
to the center of each one, were designed
by the bride, as well. "Those were a last-
minute detail that I added as a little
souvenir for our guests," says Alexandra.

"The bird and owl images were what
I had drawn on the back of our vow cards.
It was fun to see our guests mingling and
dancing with the buttons pinned on at
the end of the night."

SUCCULENT TERRARIA

Living greens on the table were a must.
Glass bowls—a select few featuring
jute wire table numbers and miniature
flag bunting—were the perfect vessels
to display Alexandra's greenery of
choice. "I've always loved the blue
and green tones of succulents and the
graphic patterns they display," she
explains. "The colors and textures have
such an earthy and hearty feel. In place
of bouquets, I decided I wanted simple,
modern terrariums as centerpieces."
An added bonus? Unlike traditional
floral centerpieces, there were no wilted
blooms to dispose of during clean-
up. "I loved that the terrariums would
continue to grow even after our wedding
was over. Our family members each
got to take one home as a special
memento of our day."

RESOURCES

Chapter 1: JESSICA & JOE

- Venue: Private home, Rolling Hills Estates, CA
- Air Plants: Air Plant Supply Co., www.airplantsupplyco.com
- Birch-Wood Frames: IKEA, www.ikea.com
- Bridal Gown: Reem Acra, www.reemacra.com
- Catering: Heirloom LA, www.heirloomla.com
- Cocktails: Pharmacie, www.pharmaciela.com
- Design/Planning: Bash, Please, www.bashplease.com
- Fabrics: International Silks and Woolens, www.internationalsilks.com
- Florals: Bash, Please, www.bashplease.com
- Guest Book: Etsy, www.etsy.com
- Invitations/Paper Design: Bash, Please, www.bashplease.com
- Linens: La Tavola, www.latavolalinen.com
- Live Klezmer Band: The Shpil, www.theshpil.com
- Luggage Tags: Staples, www.staples.com
- Metal Pots: IKEA, www.ikea.com
- Music: DJ Smiles Davis for The Flashdance, www.theflashdance.com
- Photography: Birds of a Feather, www.birdsofafeatherphoto.com
- Printing: Copperwillow, www.copperwillow.com
- Rentals/Lighting: Classic Party Rentals, www.classicpartyrentals.com
- Sweets: Cake Monkey, www.cakemonkey.com; Heirloom LA, www.heirloomla.com
- Terra-Cotta Dishes: Jamali Garden, www.jamaligarden.com
- Videography: Shark Pig, www.sharkpig.com
- Vintage Bottles: Small Masterpiece, www.smallmasterpiece.com
- Vintage Rentals: Found, www.vintage-rentals.com

Chapter 2: ANNA & COLBY

- Venue: Public park and private home, Santa Monica, CA
- Camping Tins: Supply Sergeant, Hollywood, CA, (323) 463-4730
- Catering: Heirloom LA, www.heirloomla.com
- Cocktails: Pharmacie, www.pharmaciela.com
- Design/Planning: Bash, Please, www.bashplease.com
- DJ: Ian Marshall, telepopcanada@gmail.com
- Embroidery Rings: Joann Fabric and Craft, www.joann.com

- Florals: Bash, Please, www.bashplease.com
- Hair/Makeup: Fiore Beauty, www.fiorebeauty.com
- Live Music: The Living Sisters, www.thelivingsisters.com
- Midcentury Modern Rentals: Yeah!, www.yeahrentals.com
- Paper Goods Design/Invitations: Thunderwing Press, www.thunderwingpress.com
- Photography: Charley Star, www.charleystarphoto.com
- Rentals/Lighting: Town and Country Event Rentals, www.townandcountryeventrentals.com
- Tambourines and Kazoos, Lakeshore Learning Center, www.lakeshorelearning.com
- Vintage Bottles: Small Masterpiece, www.smallmasterpiece.com
- Vintage Napkins: Rose Bowl Flea Market, www.rgcshows.com/rosebowl.aspx
- Vintage Rugs: Casa de Perrin, www.casadeperrin.com
- Wedding Cake: Vanilla Bake Shop, www.vanillabakeshop.com

Chapter 3: JESSICA & AARON

- Venue: Ace Hotel, Palm Springs, CA, www.acehotel.com/palmsprings
- Venue for Blessingmony: iT House, Pioneertown, CA, www.airbnb.com/rooms/19606
- Art Direction/Paper: Robert and Gary Williams, robertandgary.com
- Balloons: Geronimo Balloons, www.geronimoballoons.com
- Bourbon and Bowties Fashion: Forage Bow Ties, www.forage.bigcartel.com; Ban.do Accessories, www.shopbando.com
- Bridal Hair: Misty Artistry, http://www.styleseat.com/mistyspinney
- Bridal Makeup: Stacy McClure, www.makeupbystacy.com
- Bridal Party Hair/Makeup: Fiore Beauty, www.fiorebeauty.com
- Catering/Cocktails: Ace Hotel, Palm Springs, CA, www.acehotel.com/palmsprings
- Catering for Blessingmony: Heirloom LA, www.heirloomla.com
- Cocktail Napkins and Stirrers: For Your Party, www.foryourparty.com
- Custom Napkin Fabric: Spoonflower, www.spoonflower.com

- Design/Planning: Bash, Please, www.bashplease.com
- Florals: Bash, Please, www.bashplease.com
- Glass Bottles: General Bottle Supply, www.bottlesetc.com
- Hanging Planters: Etsy, www.etsy.com
- Ice Cream Sandwiches at Pool Party: Beachy Cream, www.beachycream.com
- Lighting/Rentals: Classic Party Rentals, Palm Springs, www. palmdesertclassicpartyrentals.com
- Linens: La Tavola, www.latavolalinen.com
- Live Music at Pool Party: Leftover Cuties, www.leftovercuties.com
- Live Music at Reception: Rebirth Brass Band, www.rebirthbrassband.com
- Marching Band: Palm Springs High School, schools.psusd.us/ps/
- Midcentury Modern Rentals: Yeah!, www.yeahrentals.com
- Music: Michael Antonia for The Flashdance, www.theflashdance.com
- Art Direction/Paper: Robert and Gary Williams, robertandgary.com 408-368-8531
- Parasols: Cultural Intrigue, www.culturalintrigue.com
- Photo Booth: Smilebooth, www.smilebooth.com
- Photography: Max Wanger, www.maxwanger.com
- Street Vendors Catering:
    - Sweet Lucie's Ice Cream, www.ilovelucies.com
    - Ricky's Fish Tacos, www.twitter.com/rickysfishtacos
    - Handsome Coffee, www.handsomecoffee.com
    - The Fry Girl, www.thefrygirlinc.com
    - Heirloom LA Food Truck, www.heirloomla.com
    - Let's Be Frank Dogs, www.letsbefrankdogs.com
- Tote Bags/Mail Bags: Almaden Press, www.almadenpress.com
- Videography: Shark Pig, www.sharkpig.com
- Vintage Jaguar: Klassy Kars, www.klassykarsrentalservices.com
- Water Bottles: Crate & Barrel, www.crateandbarrel.com

Chapter 4: ALEXA & MATT

- Venue: Carneros Inn, Sonoma, CA, www.thecarnerosinn.com
- Catering/Cocktails: Carneros Inn, www.thecarnerosinn.com
- Design/Planning: Bash, Please, www.bashplease.com
- DJ Music: Michael Antonia for The Flashdance, www.theflashdance.com
- Florals: Bash, Please, www.bashplease.com
- Honey Favors: Hurley Farms, www.hurleyfarms.com
- House Numbers: Home Depot, www.homedepot.com
- Invitations: Bella Figura, www.bellafigura.com

- Linens: La Tavola, www.latavolalinen.com
- Live Jazz Music: Bruno Pelletier-Bacquaert, www.brunojazz.com
- Paper Goods: Bash, Please, www.bashplease.com
- Photo Booth: Smilebooth, www.smilebooth.com
- Photography: Feather Love, www.featherlove.com
- Rentals: Wine Country Party and Events, www.winecountryparty.com
- Rock Salt Crystals: Home Depot, www.homedepot.com
- Save the Date: Bash, Please, www.bashplease.com

Chapter 5: RYAN & TIM

- Venue: Hotel Saint Cecilia, Austin, TX, www.hotelsaintcecilia.com
- Catering/Cocktails: Any Style Catering, www.anystylecatering.com
- Design/Planning: Bash, Please www.bashplease.com
- Florals: Bash, Please, www.bashplease.com
- DJ Music: Michael Antonia for The Flashdance, www.theflashdance.com
- Ice Cream Sandwiches: Cool Haus, www.eatcoolhaus.com
- Lighting: Groove Labs, www.groovelabs.com
- Live Music: Leo Rondeau, www.leorondeau.com
- Photo Booth: Smilebooth, www.smilebooth.com
- Photography: Love Me Sailor, www.lovemesailor.com
- Striped Straws: Urbanic Paper Boutique, www.urbanicdesigns.com
- Tent and Event Rentals: Marquee, www.marqueeeventgroup.com
- Videography: Shark Pig, www.sharkpig.com
- Vintage Rentals: Loot, www.lootvintagerentals.com
- Wedding Rug: Urban Outfitters, www.urbanoutfitters.com

Chapter 6: KRISTEN & JOHN

- Venue: Marvimon, Los Angeles, CA, www.marvimon.com
- Cake: Cake Monkey Bakery, www.cakemonkey.com
- Catering: Heirloom LA, www.heirloomla.com
- Cocktails: Pharmacie, www.pharmaciela.com
- Custom Matchbooks: For Your Party, www.foryourparty.com
- Design/Planning: Bash, Please, www.bashplease.com
- Florals: Bash, Please, www.bashplease.com
- Music: Michael Antonia for The Flashdance, www.theflashdance.com
- Photo Booth: The Traveling Photo Booth, www.thetravelingphotobooth.com
- Photography: Max Wanger, www.maxwanger.com

- Postcards: Anthropologie, www.anthropologie.com
- Rentals: Town and Country Event Rentals,
  www.townandcountryeventrentals.com
- Seed Bombs: Greenaid, www.greenaid.co
- Videography: Shark Pig, www.sharkpig.com

Chapter 7: BETH & GEOFF

- Venue: The Silverleaf Club, Scottsdale, AZ, www.silverleafclub.com
- Catering/Cocktails: The Silverleaf Club, www.silverleafclub.com
- Design/Planning: Bash, Please, www.bashplease.com
- Florals: Bash, Please, www.bashplease.com
- Invitations/Paper: Bash, Please, www.bashplease.com
- Linens: Classic Party Rentals, www.classicpartyrentals.com
- Live Music: Daniel Tekunoff, www.guitarmusicaz.com
- Photography: The Weaver House, www.theweaverhouse.com
- Rentals/Lighting: Classic Party Rentals, www.classicpartyrentals.com
- Videography: Son of Shark Pig, www.sonofsharkpig.com
- Wedding Favors and Bridesmaids' Bracelets: Ron Kolb,
  www.jeweleron.com

Chapter 8: SARAH & MICHAEL

- Venue: Private home, Brentwood, CA
- Burlap: Joann Fabric and Craft, www.joann.com
- Cake/Sweets: My Sweet and Saucy, www.sweetandsaucyshop.com
- Catering: Large Marge Sustainables,
  www.largemargesustainables.com
- Cocktails: Pharmacie, www.pharmaciela.com
- Design/Planning: Bash, Please, www.bashplease.com
- E.E. Cummings Poetry Book: Barnes and Noble,
  www.barnesandnoble.com
- Florals: Dandelion Ranch, www.dandelionranch.com
- Frames: Aaron Brothers, www.aaronbrothers.com
- Linens: La Tavola, www.latavolalinen.com
- Ice Cream Sandwiches: Cool Haus, www.eatcoolhaus.com
- Invitations: Urbanic Paper Boutique, www.urbanicdesigns.com
- Photo Booth: Smilebooth, www.smilebooth.com
- Photography: Charley*Star, www.charleystarphoto.com
- Rentals/Lighting: Classic Party Rentals, www.classicpartyrentals.com
- Wood Platters: Save on Crafts, www.save-on-crafts.com

Chapter 9: NINA & AMIR

- Venue: Marrakesh House, Culver City, CA,
  www.marrakeshhouse.com
- Catering: Heirloom LA, www.heirloomla.com
- Ceramic Mason Jar: CB2, www.cb2.com
- Cocktail Napkins: For Your Party, www.foryourparty.com
- Cocktails: Pharmacie, www.pharmaciela.com
- Design/Planning: Bash, Please, www.bashplease.com
- Florals: Bash, Please, www.bashplease.com
- Drag Queen Interviews: Jessica and Hunter,
  www.jessicaandhunter.com
- Lighting: The Lighter Side Wedding Event Lighting,
  www.specialeventlighting.com
- Linens: BBJ Linen, www.bbjlinen.com
- Live Music: David Daughtry Gospel Choir
  daughtrydavid@hotmail.com
- Music: Michael Antonia for The Flashdance,
  www.theflashdance.com
- Paper: Bash, Please, www.bashplease.com
- Photography: Max Wanger, www.maxwanger.com
- Rentals: Town and Country Event Rentals,
  www.townandcountryeventrentals.com
- Rug: IKEA, www.ikea.com
- Striped Bags: Sweet Lulu, www.shopsweetlulu.com
- Sweets: My Sweet and Saucy, www.sweetandsaucyshop.com
- Videography: Shark Pig, www.sharkpig.com

Chapter 10: ALEXANDRA & GREG

- Venue: Private home, Los Feliz, CA
- Catering: Heirloom LA, www.heirloomla.com
- Cocktails: Pharmacie, www.pharmaciela.com
- Custom Buttons: Busy Beaver Buttons, www.busybeaver.net
- Design/Planning: Bash, Please, www.bashplease.com
- Florals: Bash, Please, www.bashplease.com
- Glass Orbs: CB2, www.cb2.com
- Invitations: Bash, Please, www.bashplease.com
- Officiant: Jennifer Berry, jenniferberry1@me.com
- Photography: Bonnie Tsang, www.bonnietsang.com
- Rentals: Town and Country Event Rentals,
  www.townandcountryeventrentals.com